PREMIUM CAKE DECORATING

THE *I*NTERNATIONAL *C*ELEBRATION *C*AKE GALLERIA ™

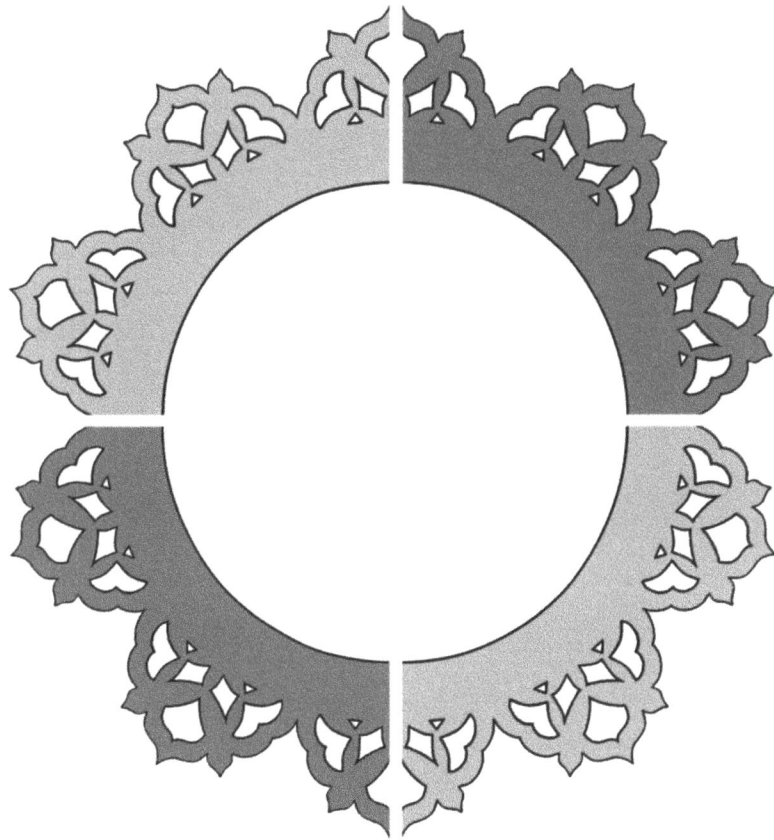

CAKE COLLAR 007

Table of Contents

Cake Collar 007

Sized for 10" round cake

FITS 10"

THE INTERNATIONAL *Celebration Cake* GALLERIA

CAKE COLLAR 007

·············· MATERIALS ··············
(for 1 round runout cake collar top and 1 round cake collar base)

Waxed paper

Scotch tape

Wilton icing Tip #3

Wilton icing Tip #4
(4 or 5 Tip #4's are recommended)

Icing bags, couplers

Royal icing (Appendix II)

Runout royal icing (Appendix III)

Two or three 10" cardboard cake circles
(to be cut to 9" diameter)

Dried fondant, fabric or foil covered
cake displayboard

Working Location:

Flat, smooth working surface where collars will remain untouched to dry.

Note: Drying may take up to two days or longer depending on humidity conditions. Please factor this into your time schedule. We recommend that you create the embellishments up to one week ahead of decorating cake.

FITS
10"

STEP 1:   RUN-OUT ICING COLLAR **TOP** AND **BASE** TEMPLATE CONSTRUCTION

- *Make photocopies of templates **Fig. 4**, **Fig. 5**, **Fig. 6**, and **Fig. 7**.*

- *Tape templates Fig. 4, Fig. 5, Fig. 6, and Fig. 7 together to create a round icing collar cake TOP template as shown below (Fig. 1).*

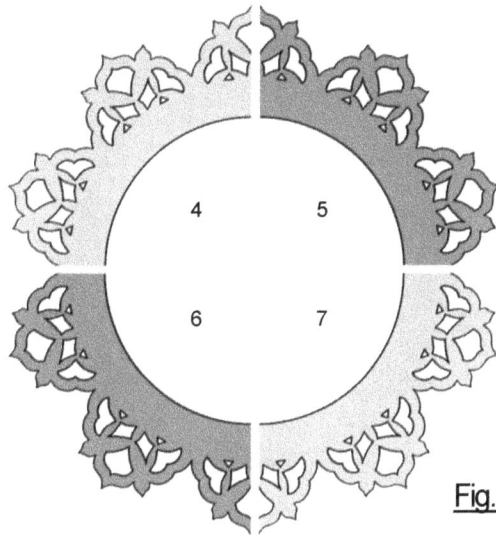

4   5

6   7

<u>Fig. 1</u>

- *Measure the resulting template to ensure that it is of correct size - ensure that the completed icing collar (Fig. 2). will securely rest on the surface of a 10" diameter cake.*

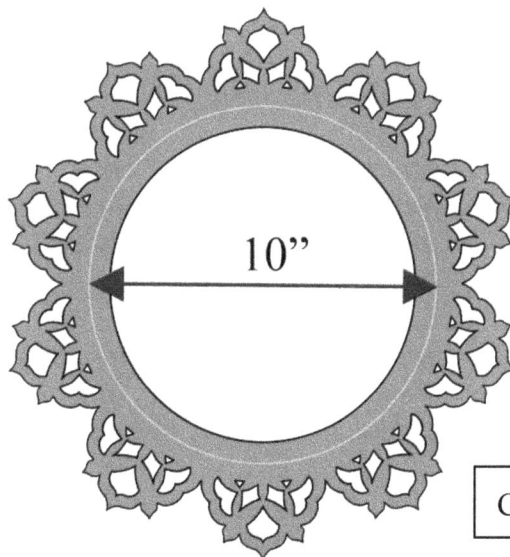

10"

CAKE TOP COLLAR

<u>Fig. 2</u>

FITS
10"

- *Make additional copies of the resulting template for backup.
  It is recommended to make one additional collar in case of breakage.*

- *Make photocopies of **Fig. 8**, **Fig. 9**, **Fig. 10**, and **Fig. 11**.
  Tape Fig. 8, Fig. 9, Fig. 10, and Fig. 11 together to create a round icing collar
  cake BASE template. Measure the interior diameter to ensure that it spans 10".*

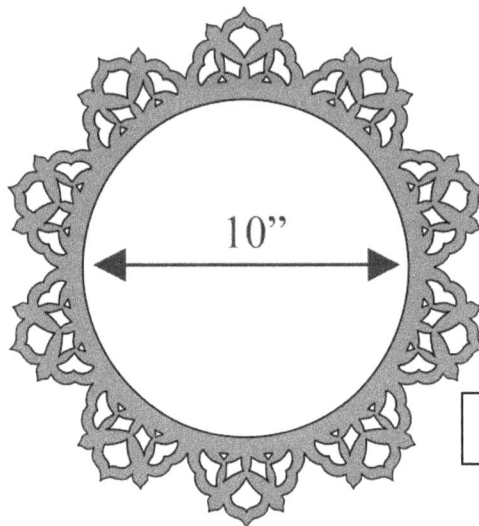

10"

CAKE BASE COLLAR

Fig. 3

Make additional copies of the resulting template for backup.

STEP 2: WORKING AREA PREPARATION

- *Designate a flat drying surface (a flat countertop for example), for creating icing collars.*

  ****Keep in mind that it is essential during the process of filling the icing collars that
  extra care is taken to prevent the wet collars from being jarred or bumped. It is
  recommended that the templates be kept stationary and thus filled from above by
  working over them and by walking around them. ****

- *Position the paper collar templates onto the counter surface. Place large sheets
  of waxed paper over each template. If more than one sheet of waxed paper is
  required per template, tape each together to become one extended sheet.*

- *Tape waxed paper lightly down onto counter surface such that each template
  beneath the waxed paper will not move. Make sure taping here is light, to reduce the
  amount of effort required when it comes time to loosen the tape to remove the dried collar.*

FITS
10"

STEP 3: OUTLINING COLLAR TEMPLATES WITH REGULAR ROYAL ICING

- *Refer to the color coding in template **Fig. 4.** Notice the black outline and gray colored interior.*

- *With this color coding in mind, you may begin work on your prepared collar templates as follows:*

  - *Using icing Tip #3 and regular royal icing, carefully outline the entire TOP cake collar and the entire BASE cake collar* (royal icing recipe: Appendix II). *Let icing outline dry for at least 30 minutes.*

STEP 4: FILLING COLLAR TEMPLATES WITH RUN-OUT ROYAL ICING

- *Make several full bags of fresh runout icing* (run-out icing recipe: Appendix III). ***Prepare the bags with Tip #4 icing tips and place them nearby (for example, stand each up in a tall glass such that the bottom of the glass prevents the icing from draining from each icing tip). Since it is difficult to estimate the amount of icing required to fill an entire template as application varies from decorator to decorator, it is recommended that should you realize as you are filling the templates that you will require more runout icing to complete the template, that you have an assistant quickly make up more icing batches well before you will need it. You must fill sections of the template continuously, allowing only a few seconds to switch to a new bag of icing. Your intent is to meld wet icing into wet icing to avoid marring, jarring, or drying marks.***

  - *Using icing Tip #4, fill in outlines with run-out royal icing* (run-out icing recipe: Appendix III)

  - *Let work dry thoroughly unmoved and untouched. Drying may take one or two full days, depending on the surrounding air humidity levels experienced at the time of the drying period.*

FITS
10"

Please ensure that the cake top template is of correct size for your intended cake size.
Measure carefully and alter the template accordingly before beginning any piped icing work.

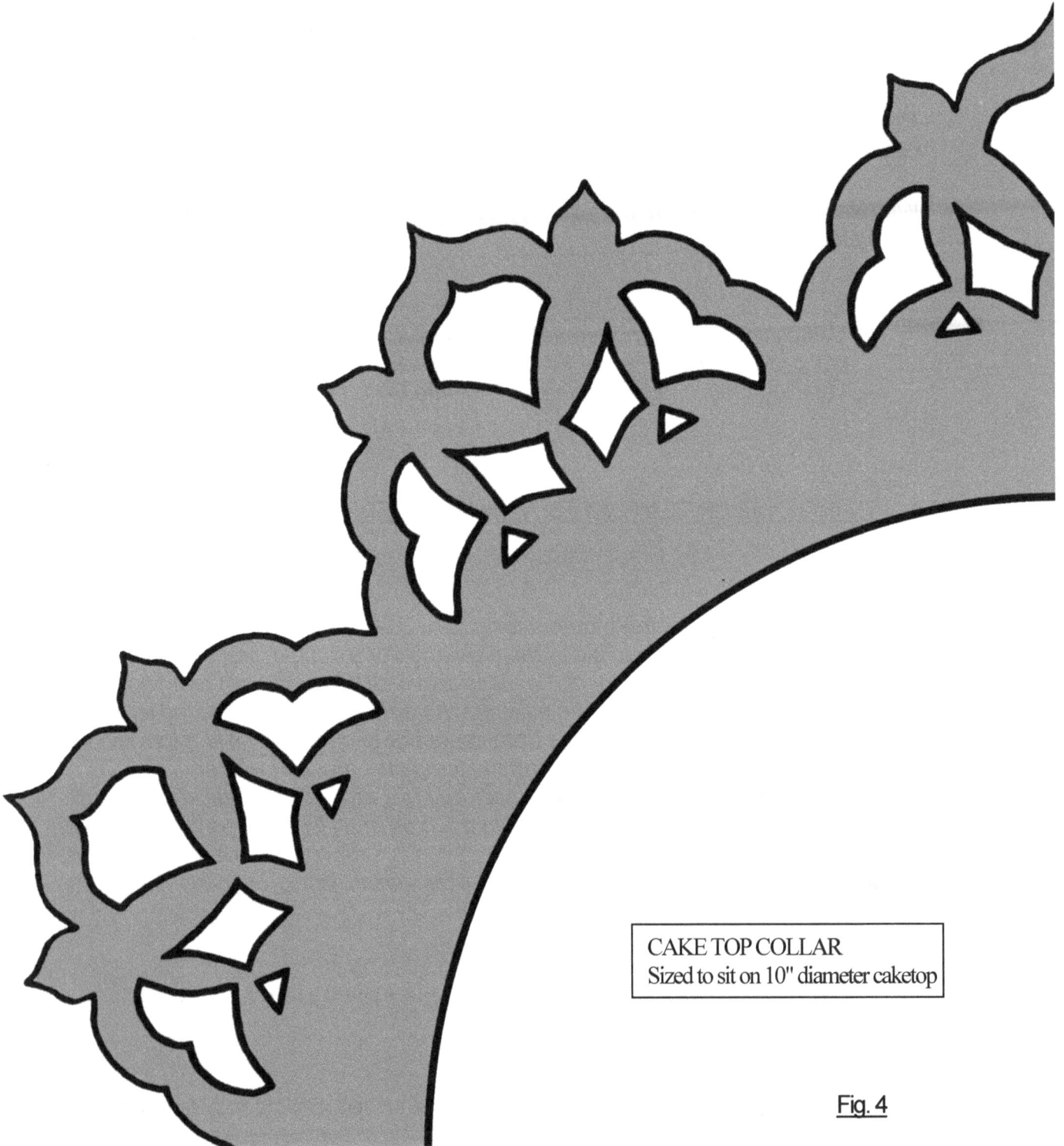

CAKE TOP COLLAR
Sized to sit on 10" diameter caketop

Fig. 4

(CAKE COLLAR 007)

FITS
10"

Please ensure that the cake top template is of correct size for your intended cake size.
Measure carefully and alter the template accordingly before beginning any piped icing work.

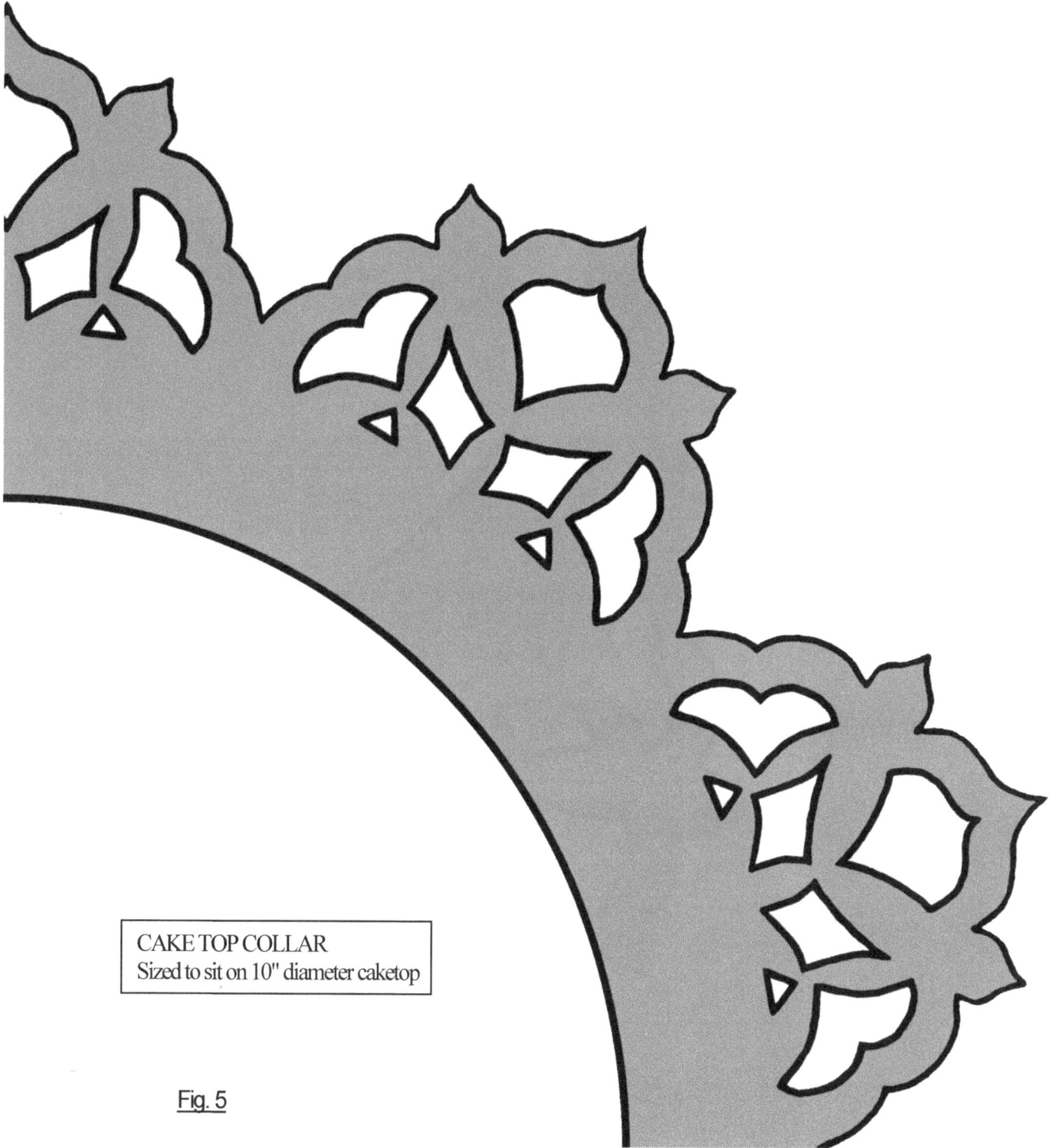

CAKE TOP COLLAR
Sized to sit on 10" diameter caketop

<u>Fig. 5</u>

(CAKE COLLAR 007)

FITS
10"

Please ensure that the cake top template is of correct size for your intended cake size.
Measure carefully and alter the template accordingly before beginning any piped icing work.

<u>Fig. 6</u>

CAKE TOP COLLAR
Sized to sit on 10" diameter caketop

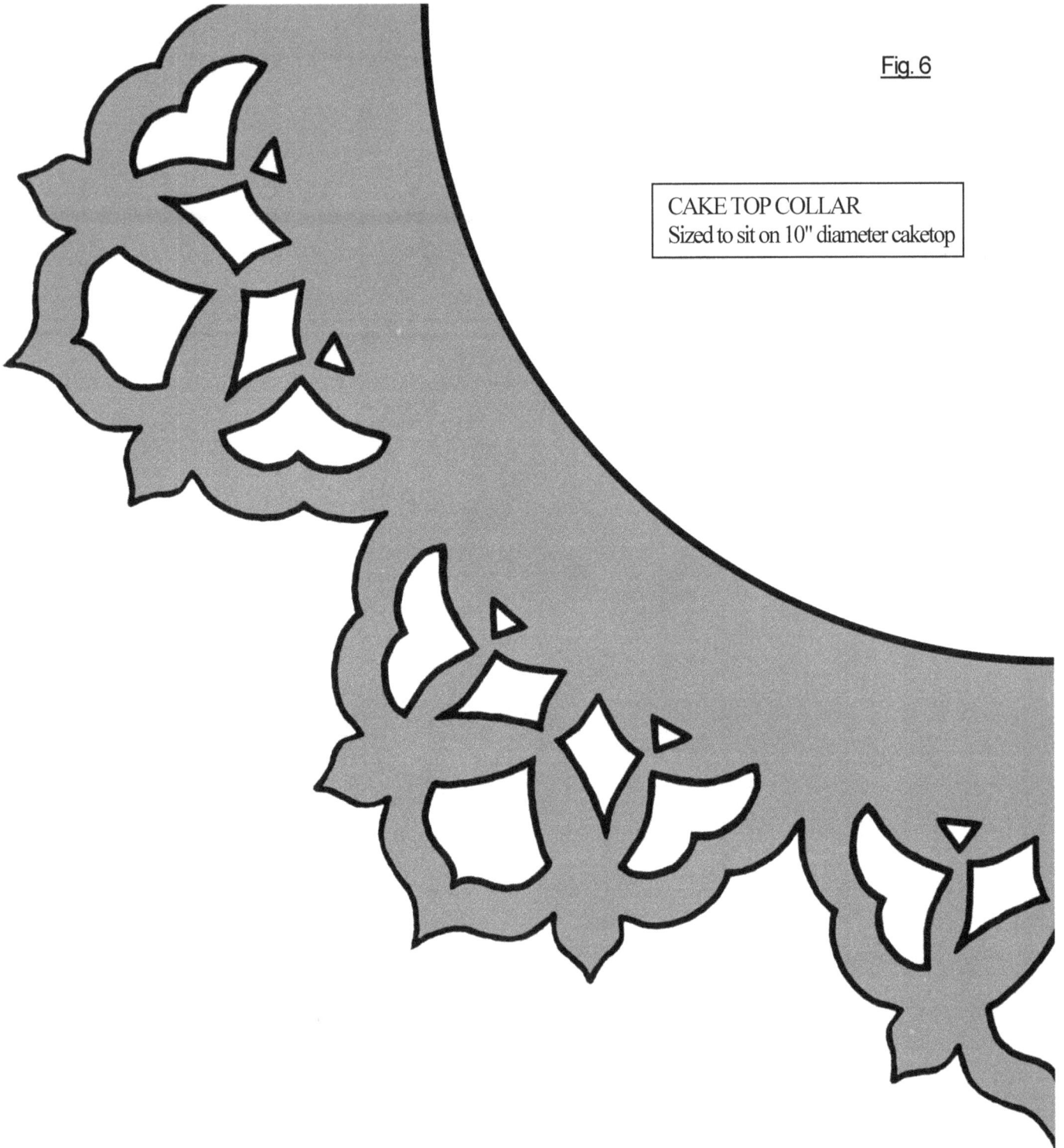

(CAKE COLLAR 007)

Please ensure that the cake top template is of correct size for your intended cake size.
Measure carefully and alter the template accordingly before beginning any piped icing work.

FITS
10"

Fig. 7

CAKE TOP COLLAR
Sized to sit on 10" diameter caketop

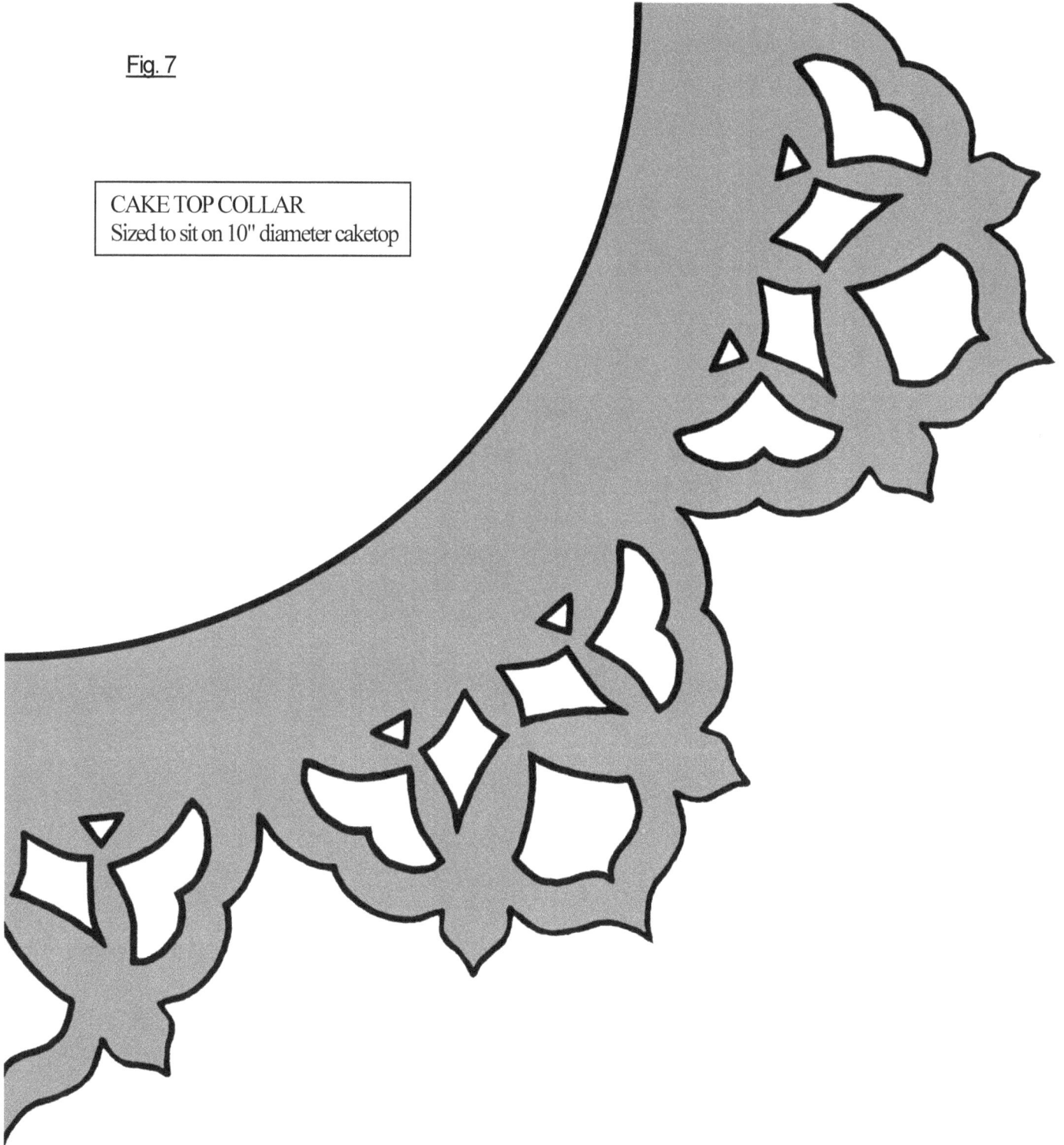

PAGE 9

FITS
10"

Please ensure that the cake base template is of correct size for your intended cake size.
Measure carefully and alter the template accordingly before beginning any piped icing work.

BASE

CAKE BASE COLLAR
Sized to fit just under a 10" diameter cake base

Fig. 8

Please ensure that the cake base template is of correct size for your intended cake size.
Measure carefully and alter the template accordingly before beginning any piped icing work.

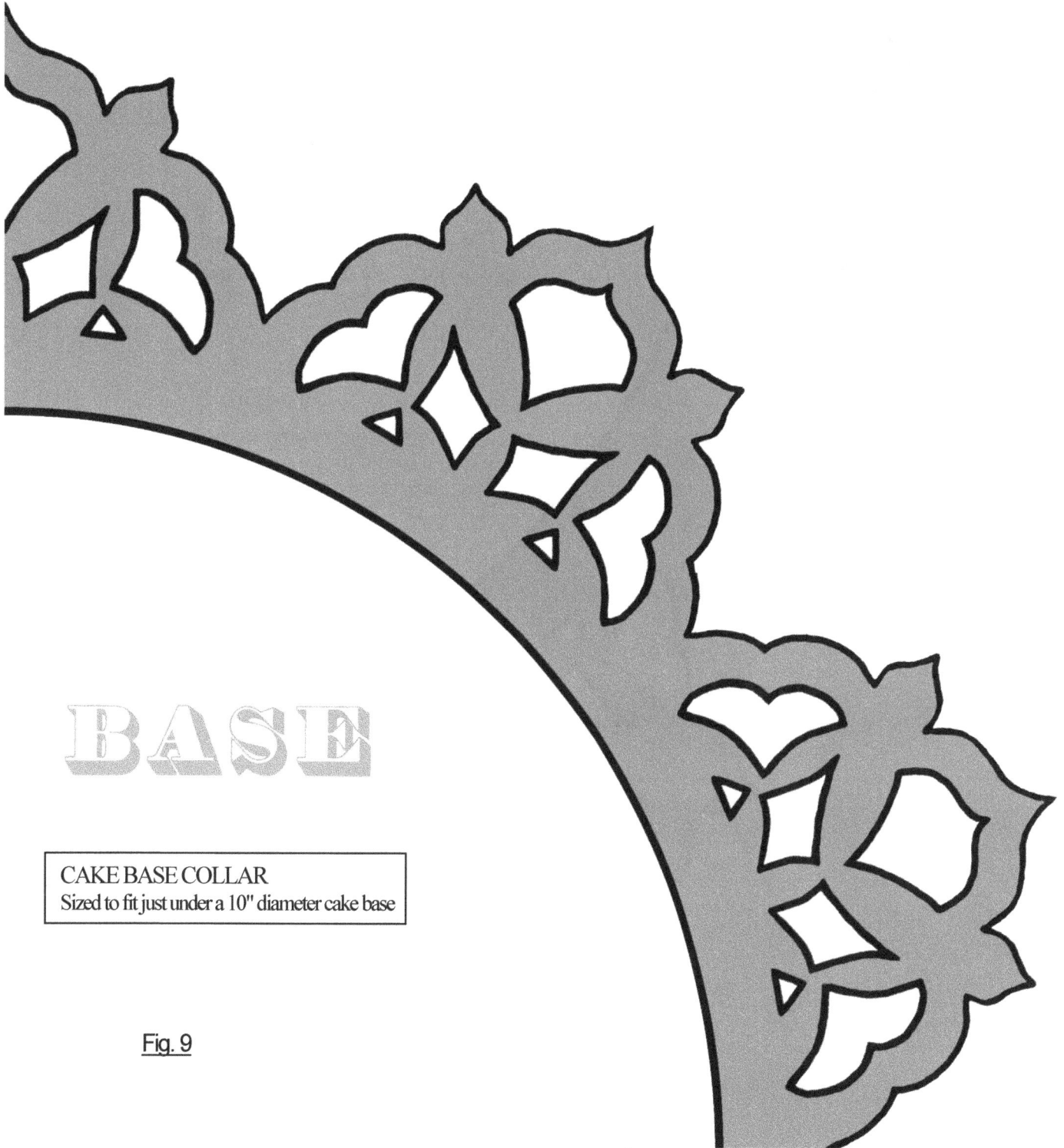

FITS
10"

BASE

CAKE BASE COLLAR
Sized to fit just under a 10" diameter cake base

Fig. 9

(CAKE COLLAR 007)

FITS
10"

Please ensure that the cake base template is of correct size for your intended cake size.
Measure carefully and alter the template accordingly before beginning any piped icing work.

<u>Fig. 10</u>

CAKE BASE COLLAR
Sized to fit just under a 10" diameter cake base

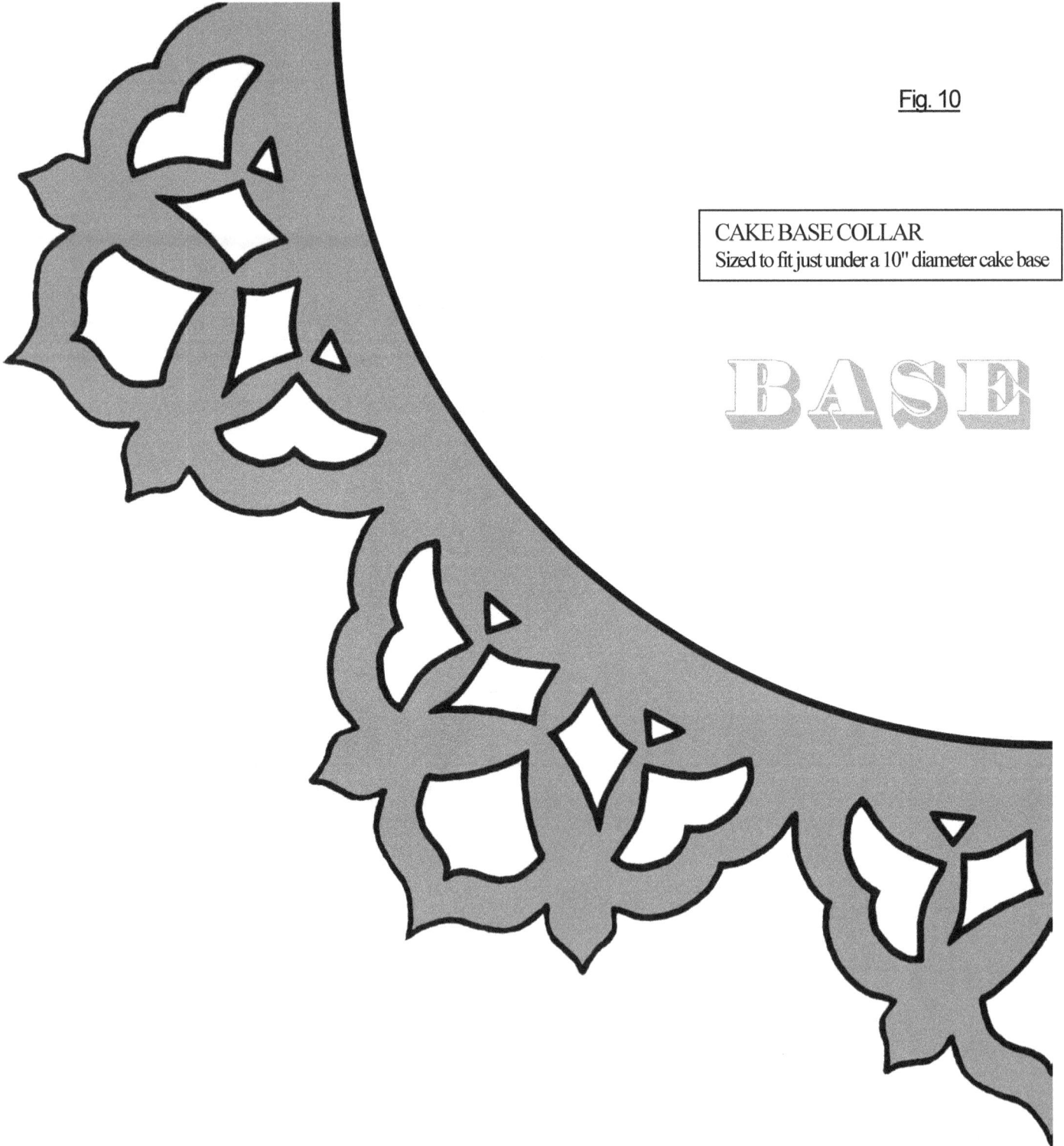

BASE

(CAKE COLLAR 007)

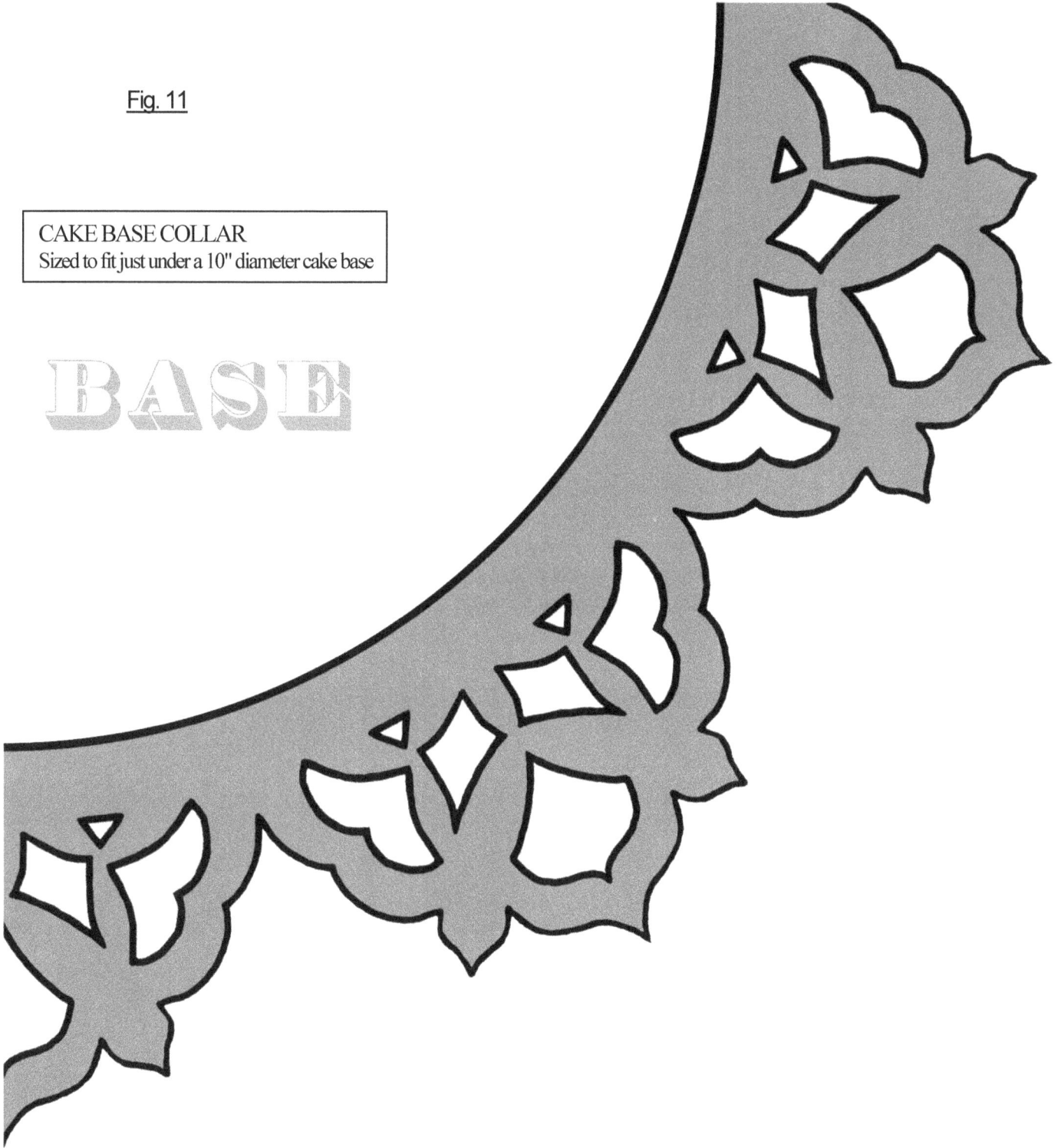

Please ensure that the cake base template is of correct size for your intended cake size.
Measure carefully and alter the template accordingly before beginning any piped icing work.

FITS
10"

Fig. 11

CAKE BASE COLLAR
Sized to fit just under a 10" diameter cake base

BASE

FITS
10"

STEP 5: REMOVING DRIED ICING COLLARS FROM WAXED PAPER

- *Carefully remove the tape holding the waxed paper sheets to the counter top.*

- *Slide one waxed paper sheet/ dried collar down the countertop away from remaining collar(s).*

- *Position this collar with one portion of its outside edge along the outer edge of the countertop.*

- *With the fingers of one hand guiding and holding the waxed paper sheet/dried cake collar to the counter, carefully remove the waxed paper from the dried collar with your remaining hand, by gently pulling the waxed paper edge downward, and pulling the waxed paper taught against the edge of the counter. The waxed paper should peel easily away from the collar if it has been allowed to fully dry.*

Carefully rotate the waxed paper sheet holding the dried collar along the flat surface of the countertop as required, pulling the waxed paper away from the collar edges as described above, until the entire collar has been freed from the waxed paper.

FITS
10"

STEP 6: POSITIONING TOP AND BASE COLLARS ON CAKE

- *Position your cake displayboard on a flat surface nearby*

- *Slide the waxed paper holding the freed cake collar base, to the edge of the counter. Extend a portion of the collar over the edge of the counter. Let the waxed paper hang downwards.*

- *Spread your fingers under the portion of the collar extending over the counter, and guide the icing collar outwards from the counter edge until you have it evenly balanced and resting on all of your fingertips.*

- *Carefully transport the collar to the cake display board and position.*

- *Cut two or three cardboard cake circles to approximately 9" in diameter. Stack these cake circles in the center of the displayboard. These cake circles will bear the weight of the iced cake and thus should sit somewhat higher than the cake collar. Ensure that with the added weight, that these circles will not allow the cake to rest on the runout collar base. Place a piece of tape between each cake circle and the displayboard for additional security.*

- *Center fondant covered cake (already on its own foil cakeboard) into the center of the cake collar base, onto the stacked cake circles.*

- *Add decorative ribbon or icing beading around the base of the cake to cover any existing gap.*

- *Using icing Tip #3 or larger, place several beads of royal icing onto the cake surface, approximately 1/2" from the cake edge around the circumference of the cake.*

- *Remove and transport the remaining cake top collar from the waxed paper to the cake as previously instructed.*

Center collar onto cake top, identically matching the position of the cake collar base.

Cake Collar 007 is available in various sizes.

Choose from 6", 7", 8", 9", 10", 12", 14", 16", 18".

www.InternationalCelebrationCakeGalleria.com

Purchase ... Print ... Create!

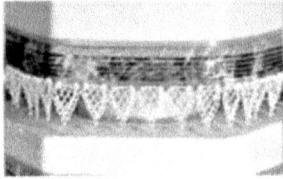

Royal Icing

for Piped Icing Embellishments

. dries hard
. commonly used for decorative piping work on cakes covered in fondant icing
. additionally used for creating icing shapes and embellishments to be attached to cakes
. ideal for very fine and intricate decorative piping work
. although dried, can often be removed from fondant at serving
. when dried, holds tightly as an adhesive when adhering icing pieces, lace or objects to fondant
. can easily be tinted or colored
. simple and quick to make, requiring only a small number of inexpensive ingredients

(2X this recipe will fill one large Wilton icing bag)

1 1/3 Cup powdered icing sugar
1 egg white
1/8 tsp of white color powder or liquid white coloring
(for brilliant white icing or to lighten colored icing)
Powder coloring or liquid coloring or color paste as required

- Mix icing sugar and egg white with mixing spoon to fold dry ingredient into wet. Then beat at low speed with electric mixer until blended.
- Follow below instructions to color the icing, then beat at high speed until very glossy and stiff peaks form.
- Add small amounts of powdered icing sugar if required, until the icing appears to be strong enough that if piped through a nozzle, it will hold the resulting pattern. If it seems you have added a little too much icing sugar and the icing appears too stiff, add a few drops of water. Working this way to get the correct consistency will not significantly hurt the icing drying strength.

Store additional icing to be used in a sealed container in refrigerator. For optimum freshness use this refrigeration method only temporarily for several hours as you work through bags of icing during a project.

For brilliant white icing:

Add as much white color powder (1/8 tsp at a time) or add liquid white coloring in small amounts as required until icing becomes a bright white. Without adding the whitener, the icing will appear yellowy as it dries.

For colored icing:

Add as much color powder, color liquid or color paste as required. Icing will not appear to dry yellowy with this coloring in it. Adding whitener is not necessary unless you desire a lighter pastel version of your color.

Runout Icing

for Cake Collars and Solid Icing Embellishments
(templates must be preoutlined with dried piped royal icing)

....

. dries hard
. commonly used for creating icing shapes and structural embellishments to be attached to cakes
. can often be removed from cakes at serving
. can easily be tinted or colored
. simple and quick to make, requiring only a small number of inexpensive ingredients

....

(This recipe will fill one large Wilton icing bag to a manageable size)

2 Cups powdered icing sugar
1 large egg white
1 small egg white
1/4 tsp of white coloring powder
(for brilliant white icing) OR
Coloring powder to add as required
Several tablespoons of water

- Mix icing sugar and egg white with mixing spoon to fold dry ingredient into wet.
  Then beat at low speed with electric mixer until blended.

For brilliant white icing:

Add as much white color powder (1/4 tsp at a time) until icing becomes a bright white.
Without adding the whitening powder, the icing will appear yellow as it dries. You may
use liquid white coloring for additional brightness, but use it sparingly as it contains
glycerine and will attract moisture to embellishments while drying. It is recommended that
if liquid coloring is utilized, to let your decorations dry for an extended time before removing
from waxed paper.

For colored icing:

Sparingly add small amounts of coloring powder until desired icing hue and color strength
has been reached. Icing will not appear to dry yellow with this coloring powder in it. Adding
white color powder is not necessary unless you desire a lighter pastel version of your color
or require a color adjustment.

Next, beat icing at high speed until very glossy and stiff peaks form. Add water to the
icing a tablespoon at a time until the icing appears to run off the lifted beaters like
corn syrup, and therefore the icing running down into the bowl does not hold its shape.

Place your prepared icing bag with fastened piping tip into a tall glass, nozzle down. Open
the icing bag top wide, then pour the icing in the bowl into the bag. Promptly begin filling in
your dried piped royal icing preoutlined templates, gently guiding and squeezing the bag to
push the icing out. The icing should immediately flatten into your preoutlined template without
any lines. Should any bubbles appear, simply dip a finger into a glass of water and gently
rub/dissolve the area to smoothness. Should you find the icing is not settling immediately
without lines, try holding the lower portion of the bag under a stream of hot tap water for a
few seconds to melt the icing or remove the icing from the bag and add additional water.
Place the refreshed icing into a new icing bag to resume the runout process.

Beverley Way

Founder, President and CEO, Beverley Way Designs Inc. USA

www.beverleywaycollection.com
www.internationalcelebrationcakegalleria.com

With a keen sense for structure, dimension, and design, Beverley studied art at McMaster University, Hamilton, Ontario, Canada on several scholarships. She holds a Bachelor of Science in Health Sciences Biology and a Bachelor of Arts in Business Administration and Economics, both from Brock University, Ontario, Canada. Beverley also attended Mohawk College, Canada, for additional business studies. She is author of The Beverley Way Collection WEDDING CAKES Book 1, Beverley Way Collection WEDDING CAKES Book 2, ELEGANT DREAM WEDDING CAKES (*A Collection of Memorable Small Cake Designs, Simple Techniques with Stunning Results*), and is concept artist and leader for numerous business projects to be developed. A number of celebrity style wedding cake designs by Beverley Way have featured in bridal magazines abroad.

Upon a move to the USA, Beverley founded Beverley Way Designs in 1995, and then incorporated the company in 2008. The company's first online division www.beverleywaycollection.com was developed and launched in 2008. This division is an ecommerce platform designed to showcase the work of Beverley Way and the impressive work of cake artists worldwide. The site presents re-creatable wedding cake ideas from the very small and simple, to the jaw-dropping multi-tiered cake. Patterns and templates to recreate each cake featured on beverleywaycollection.com are available for immediate purchase. Purchase ... Print ... Create!

The International Celebration Cake Galleria, the company's second online division located at www.internationalcelebrationcakegalleria.com was developed and launched in 2012.

APPENDIX IV

View additional books and downloadable instructions provided by
The International Celebration Cake Galleria
@

www.InternationalCelebrationCakeGalleria.com

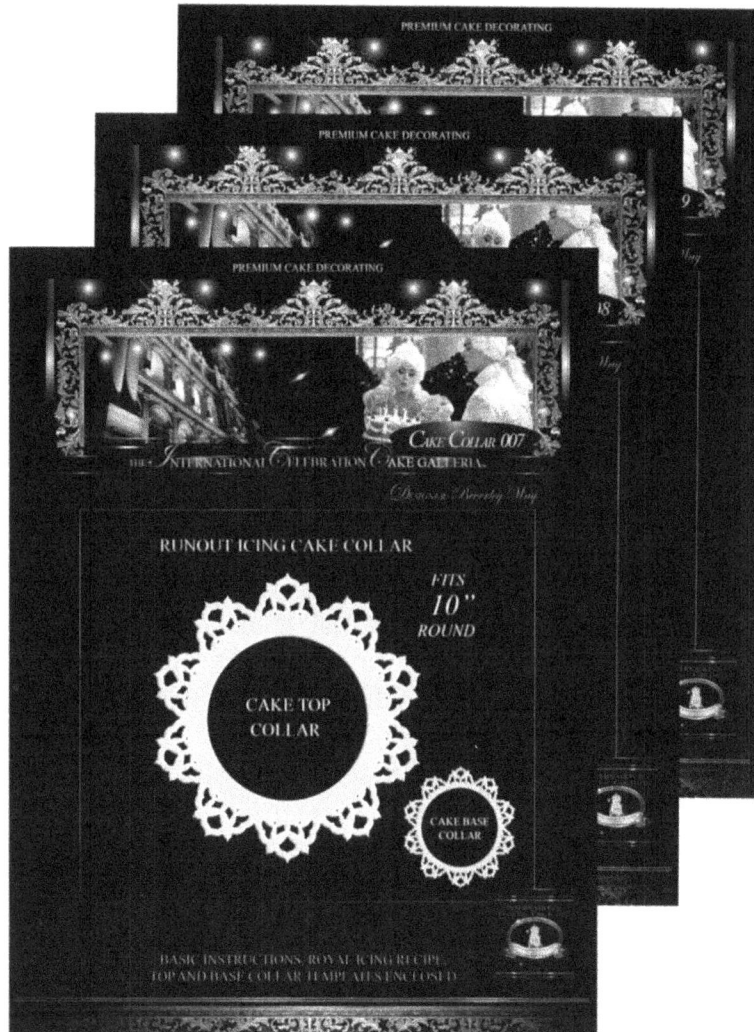

Help us to improve our products!

Submit your comments to:

ProductDevelopment@InternationalCelebrationCakeGalleria.com

APPENDIX V

<u>**DISCLAIMER**</u>

The International Celebration Cake Galleria is a division of Beverley Way Designs Inc.

Beverley Way Designs, Inc. strives to provide easy-to-follow professional quality instructions for all cake designs provided by The International Celebration Cake Galleria. However, it is up to the customer, cake decorator, or baker to perform careful work and skill to arrive at each final result. Measurements and details may require variations depending on the materials available to those recreating our provided concepts. There is no guarantee or warranty of any kind from The International Celebration Cake Galleria attached to your purchase of this instructional booklet and its contents.

BEVERLEY WAY DESIGNS INC., HEREBY DISCLAIMS ANY IMPLIED WARRANTY AT LAW. WE DISCLAIM ANY WARRANTY OF MERCHANTABILITY OR FITNESS FOR A PARTICULAR PURPOSE.

All steps and images provided to recreate Cake Collar 007 are:
© Copyright Beverley Way Designs Inc.

www.ingramcontent.com/pod-product-compliance
Lightning Source LLC
Chambersburg PA
CBHW080537030426
42337CB00023B/4769